I Love Spring!

Girl's Activity Book

Kids' Activity Books

Vol. 3

Sherley Grace

simply DONE
PUBLISHING

Montreal, Quebec Canada

Dedication

To my amazing children, you bring me great joy. I am so grateful for you both. Love you forever! God bless.

I Love Spring! Girl's Activity Book
Volume 3 – Kids' Activity Books Series
Created By Sherley Grace

ISBN – 978-1-988225-30-2

simply
DONE
PUBLISHING
Montreal, Quebec Canada

www.DiscoverYourPowerStrategies.com
SherleyGrace@DiscoverYourPowerStrategies.com

This book belongs to:

_____

With love from:

_____

Welcome!

Welcome to Volume 3 in the #1 Best-Selling Kids' Activity Books Series, entitled "I Love Spring! Girl's Activity Book." I am so excited that you are here!

You'll find over 50 fun, spring-themed activities in these next few pages!

What You Will Need

All you need to get started is your imagination, a pencil, colour pencils and/or crayons and a ruler. I don't recommend using markers, as the ink may bleed through the paper.

Get ready to spend fun times colouring, drawing, connecting the dots, making your way through mazes, testing your memory, and solving many other puzzles too.

What Activity Books Would You Love To Have Next?

I am always looking for topic ideas for upcoming Activity Books in the "I Love" Series. So, if you have any ideas, be sure to send me an email. I'll read all of the suggestions and create future Activity Books based on the most popular topics.

I'd also like to know what you and your parents like most about this Activity Book. I'd love to see some of your completed pages or even pictures of you having fun, completing some of the activities.

Perhaps your Mom or Dad can email me at **SherleyGrace@DiscoverYourPowerStrategies.com** with your comments, ideas, and pictures. I can't wait to hear from you!

Sneak Peek – Just For You!

If you like this activity book, you are going to love the next Activity Book in this Series. It's called, **"I Love Fairies! Girl's Activity Book."**

You'll meet and have some magical moments completing fun activities with many wonderful fairies, including Anna the Animal Fairy, Trixie the Tooth Fairy, Chrissy the Christmas Fairy, Bianca the Bedtime Fairy and many others too!

At the end of this book, I've actually included a **sneak peek**, with some bonus Fairy Funtastic activities, just for you. Be sure to check it out!

Big hugs to you,

Sherley

Hide And Seek

It looks like Mr. Owl has hidden several items for you to find. Look at the list below, and circle in the picture, each item that you find.

FIND THE FOLLOWING ITEMS:

2 rain boots , BBQ, bird, fire, mouse, mushroom, plate with fruit, snowman, soccer ball, spring hat, sunflower, tulip

Connect The Dots – Splashing Bear!

Using a pencil, connect the dots, in order from 1 to 76. What did you create? Now, colour your picture using your crayons or colour pencils.

Gazing Princess

Grab your favourite colour pencils or crayons, and have fun colouring this pretty picture!

Rhyming Time

Look at the pictures below. Using a pencil and ruler, draw lines to match the pictures that rhyme.

Find the Pairs

Circle and draw a line from one rain boot to its match to create the pair. One rain boot does not have a match. Can you find it?

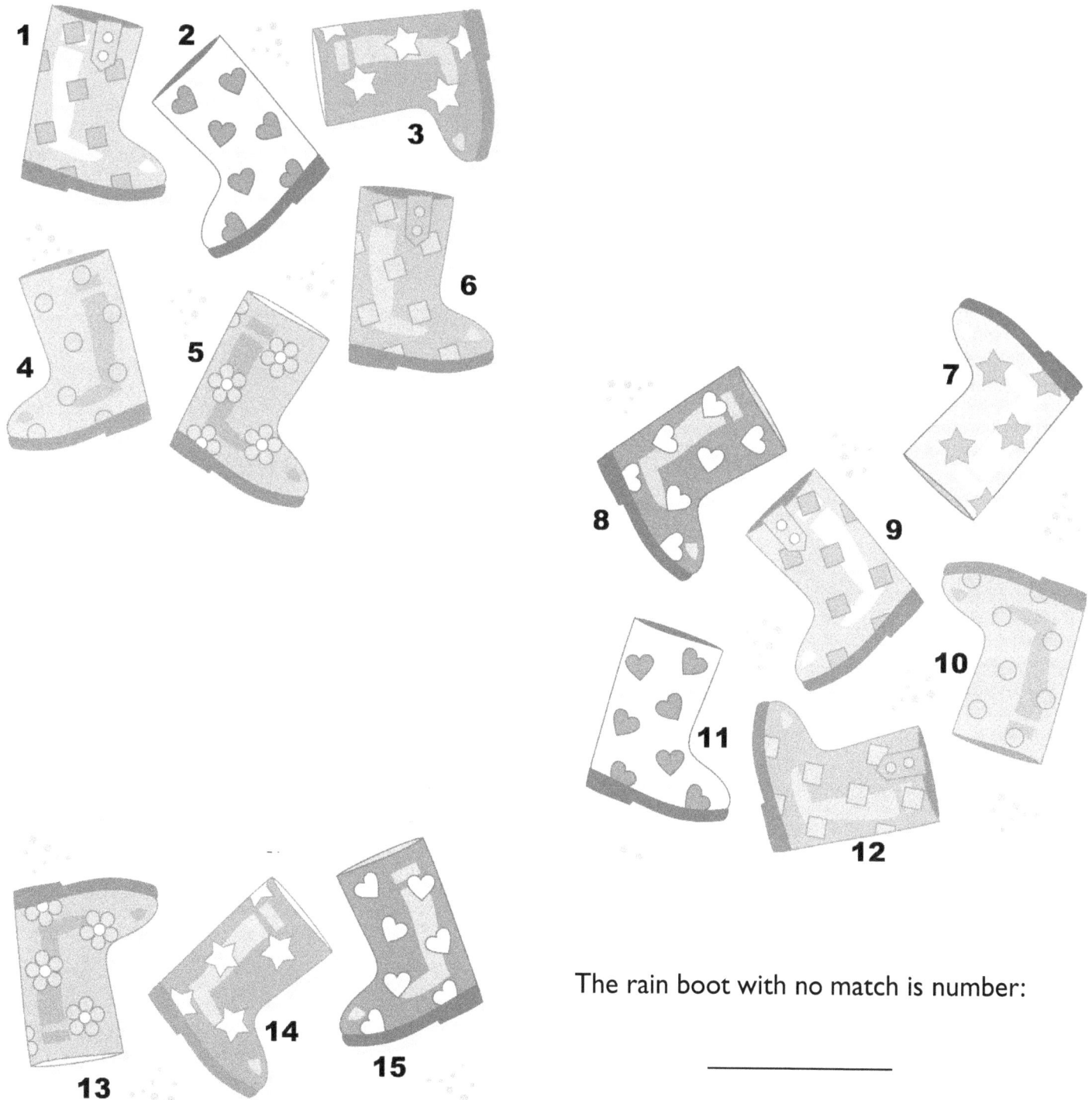

1

2

3

4

5

6

7

8

9

10

11

12

13

14

15

The rain boot with no match is number:

_____

Springtime Showers

Look closely at the images below. Can you find 10 differences? Use a pencil or colour pencil to circle the differences you find.

Springtime Sudoku

Using your colour pencils or crayons, complete the puzzle below. An image must appear only once in every 2x2 square, row and column.

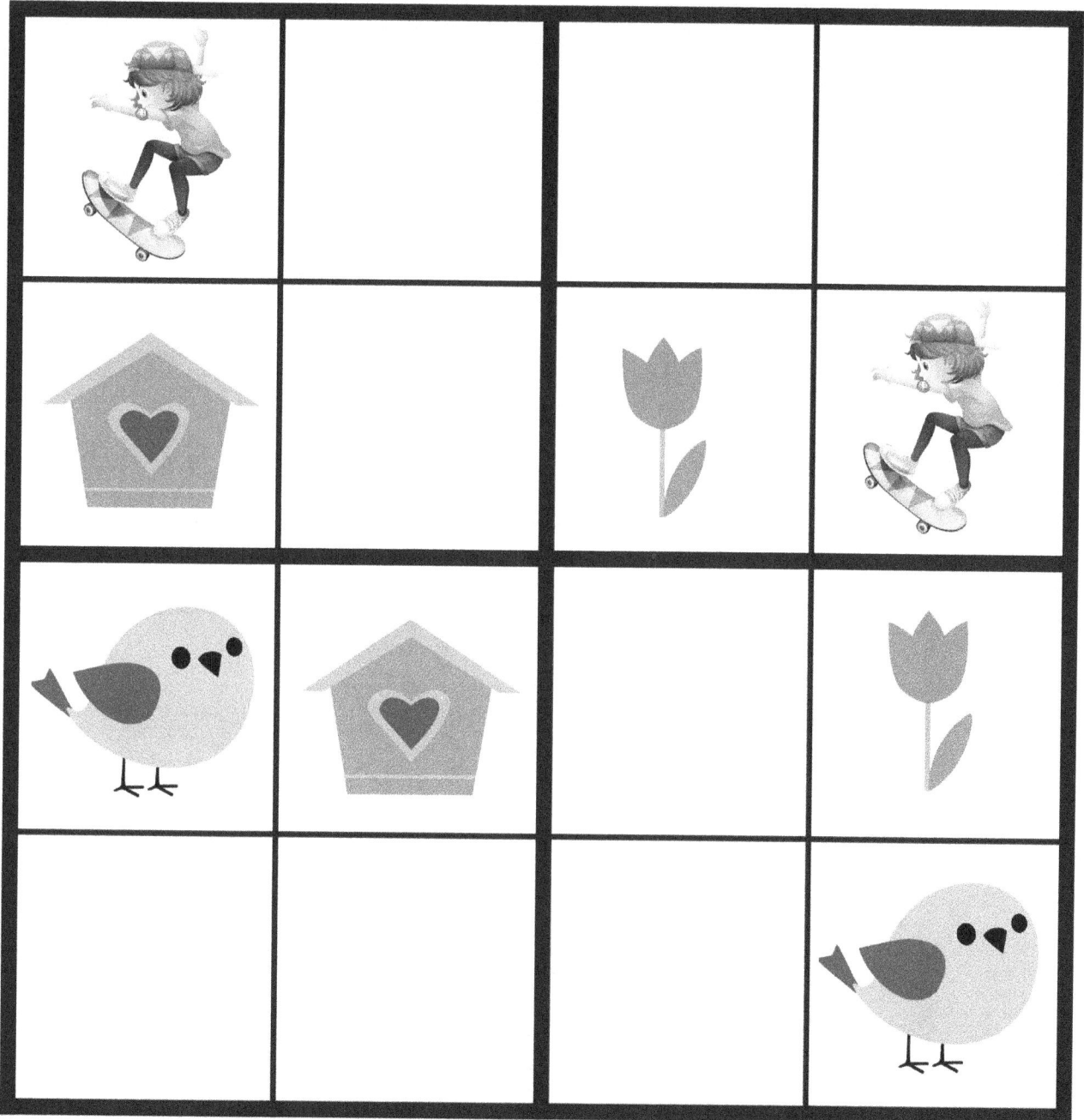

Floral Maze

Using a pencil or colour pencil, make your way through the flower maze. Begin at the "START" point, and make your way through the maze until you get to the "End" point.

Start

End

Flower Market

Grab your favourite colour pencils or crayons, and have fun colouring this beautiful springtime picture!

Tic-Tac-Toe

Find a friend, grab some pencils, and have fun playing Tic-Tac-Toe!

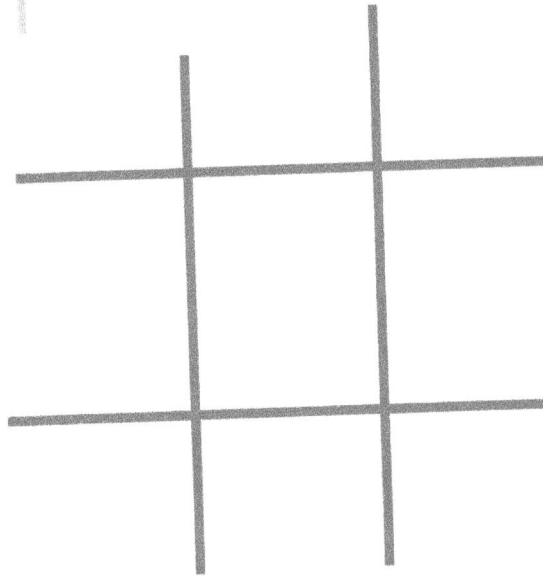

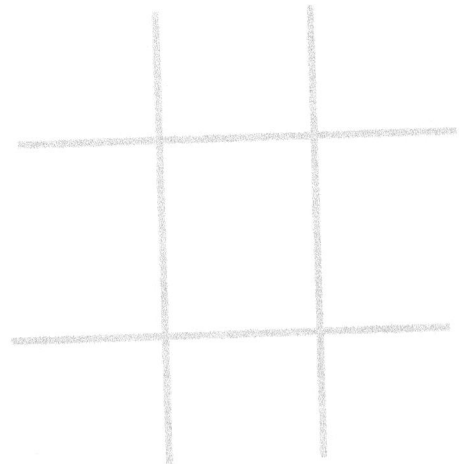

Spring Bugs

How many of the spring bugs can you find? Find and circle each of the bug names in the puzzle below, using a pencil or colour pencil.

```
J U X H V S T D V N B B F A X C
X P O U S Y L W F Q T R O W X
O T B U T T E R F L Y L O J B O
D C A T E R P I L L A R G Q K O
R X S P I D E R I P V K N L E F
R L A D Y B U G R K J F R E E V
M B H U R E Y H A E Q L B L Q K
L A U G Y M Q G Q N O Y T W Z R
I H S T V S N A I L T E Q P G N
P P O R I O H N T R E K X B B Y
J C P L S H V M O B X F O N S V
```

ANT
BEE
FLY
BUTTERFLY
BEETLE
LADYBUG
FROG
SNAIL
SPIDER
CATERPILLAR

Rainy Day

Look carefully at each group of rain boots and umbrellas. Using a pencil or colour pencil and a ruler, draw a line from each image to its shadow.

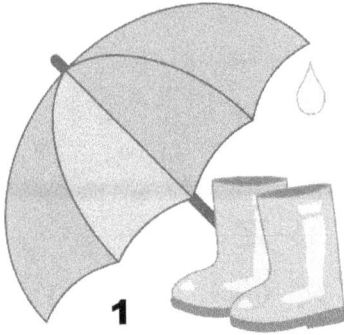

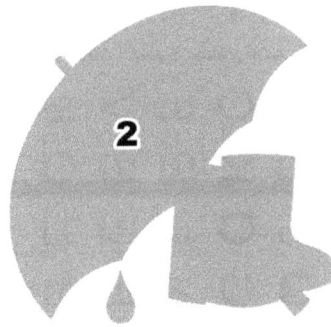

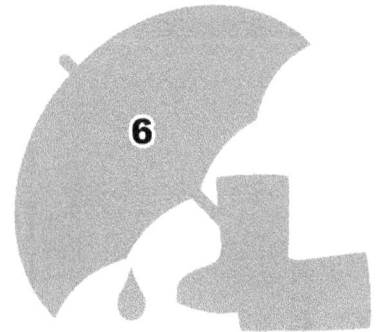

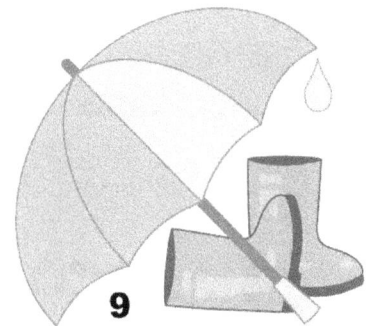

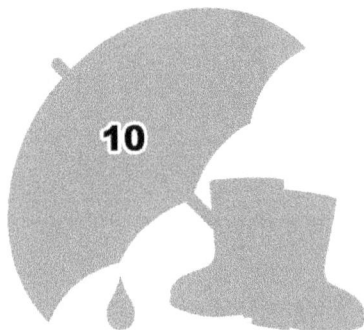

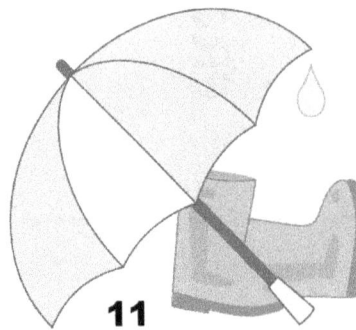

1

2

3

4

5

6

7

8

9

10

11

12

Bird Town Memory Game

Examine this picture carefully. Then turn the page, and see how many questions you can answer without looking back at the picture!

Bird Town Memory Game – Questions

Now that you have examined each item on the previous page, let's see how many questions you can answer without peeking at the picture.

1. How many birds are in the picture?

2. How many birds are facing left?

3. How many birdhouses are there?

4. What are the shapes of the doorways of the birdhouses?

5. How many pickets does the fence have?

6. What do you see in front of the fence?

7. Name the shape of some of the birds' wings

8. How many branches are in the picture?

9. Is there a tree trunk in the picture? Yes or no?

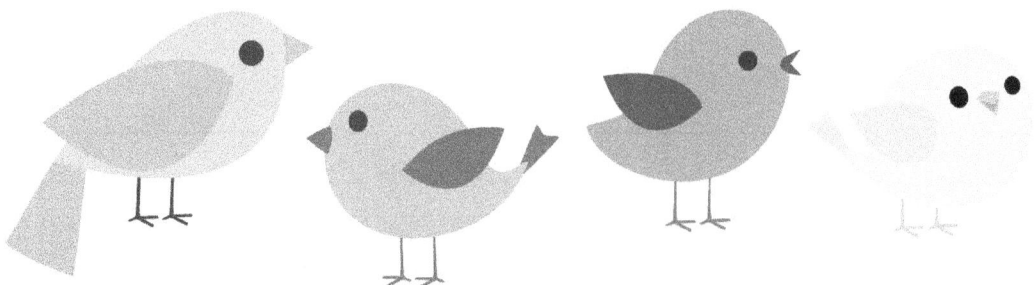

Spring Flowers

Grab your favourite colour pencils or crayons, and have fun colouring these beautiful spring flowers!

Connect The Dots – It's Springtime!

Using a pencil, connect the dots, in order from 1 to 61. What did you create? Now, colour your picture using your crayons or colour pencils.

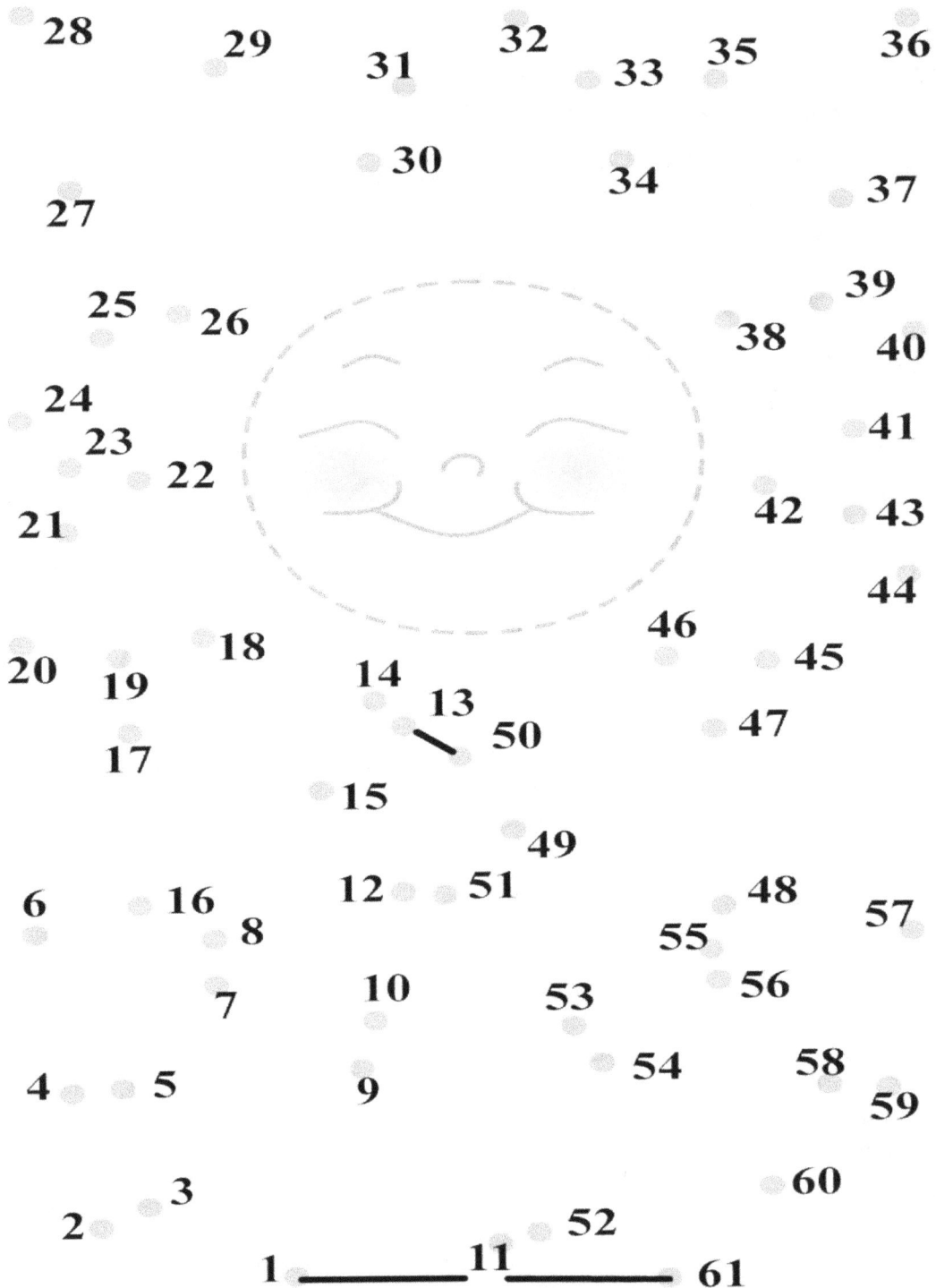

28   29   31   32   33   35   36

30   34   37

27

25   26   39
38   40

24
23   41
22

21   42   43

44

46

18   45

20   19   14   13
50   47

17   15

49

6   16   12   51   48   57
8   55

10   53   56
7

54   58

4   5   9   59

3   60

2   52

1 ——————— 11 ——————— 61

16

Buzzing Bee – Find 8 Differences

Look closely at the images below. Can you find 8 differences? Use a pencil or colour pencil to circle the differences you find.

Birdie Village

Grab your favourite colour pencils or crayons, and fill in the blanks using one of the images numbered from 1 to 5. Next to each number in the grid, write the number of the missing image. There should only be one of each type of picture in each row and column.

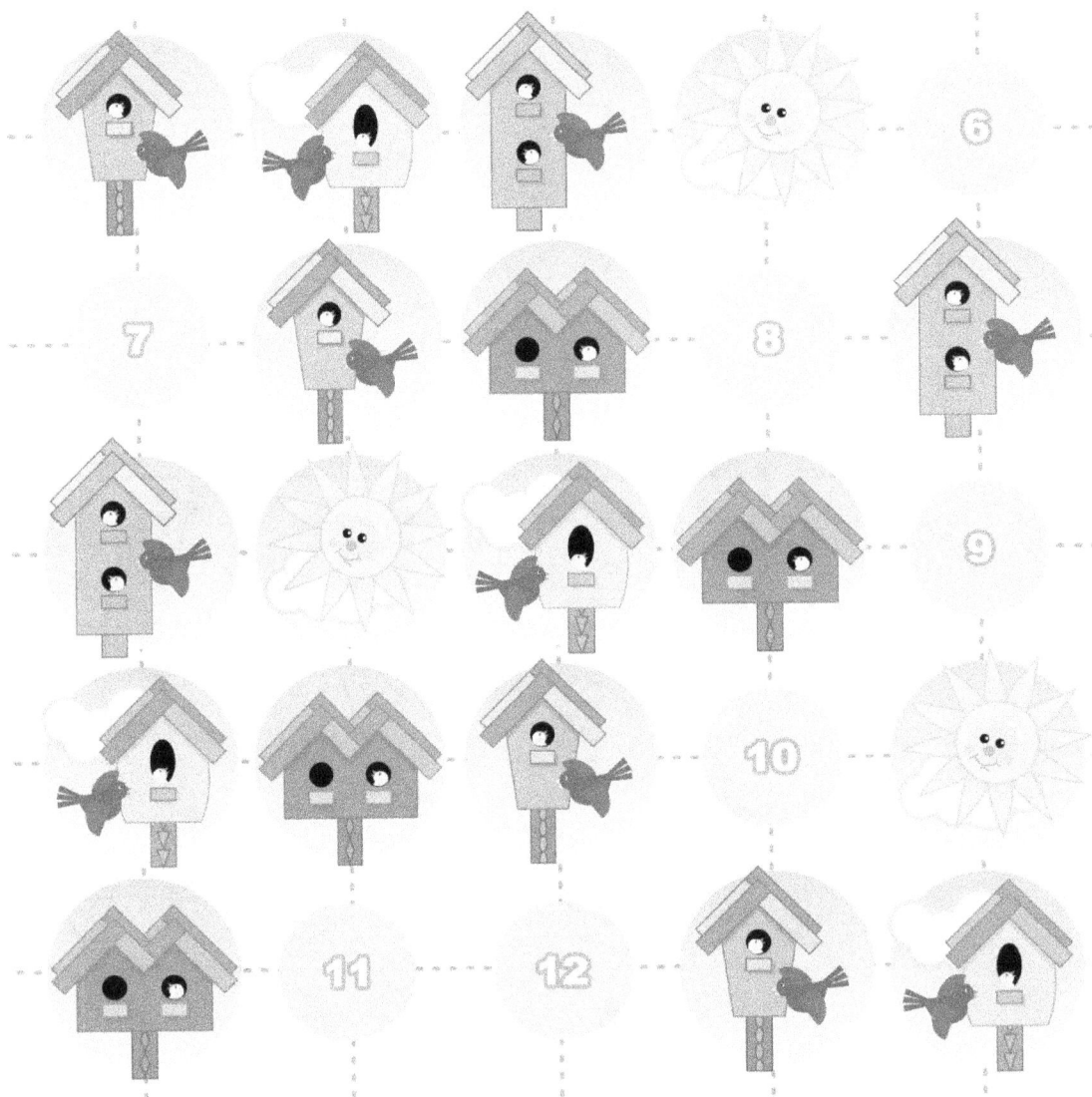

Mirror Image Mushrooms

Find the exact mirror image for each row of mushrooms.   Using a pencil, draw a line from each row of mushrooms to its mirror image.

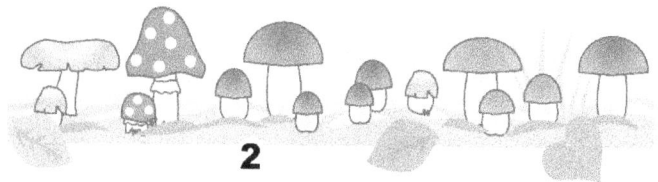

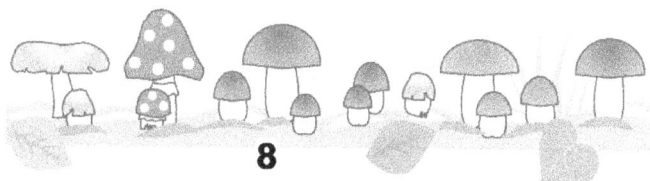

1

2

3

4

5

6

7

8

Name That Flower

Match the flower to its name. Using a pencil or colour pencil and a ruler, draw a line from each flower to its name.

A.

1. Lily

B.

2. Sunflower

C.

3. Bird of Paradise

D.

4. Rose

E.

5. Daffodil

F.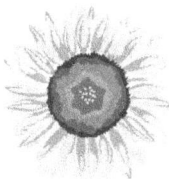

6. Tulip

I Love To Colour – Spring Mouse

Using your crayons or colour pencils, colour this beautiful springtime mouse.

Buzz Maze

This little bee is hungry. Help her make her way through the maze to the nectar. Use a pencil or colour pencil to trace the path from the bee to the center of the flower.

Twin Butterflies

Only two of the butterflies are identical. Find and circle the two butterflies that are the same.

5

Secret Spring Message

Use the secret code chart below to find the special springtime message that's just for you!

A	B	E	F	G	H	I	L	M	N

O	P	R	S	W	Y

Spring Crossword

Using a pencil and the hints below, complete the Crossword Puzzle. For additional clues, be sure to look at the list of possible words.

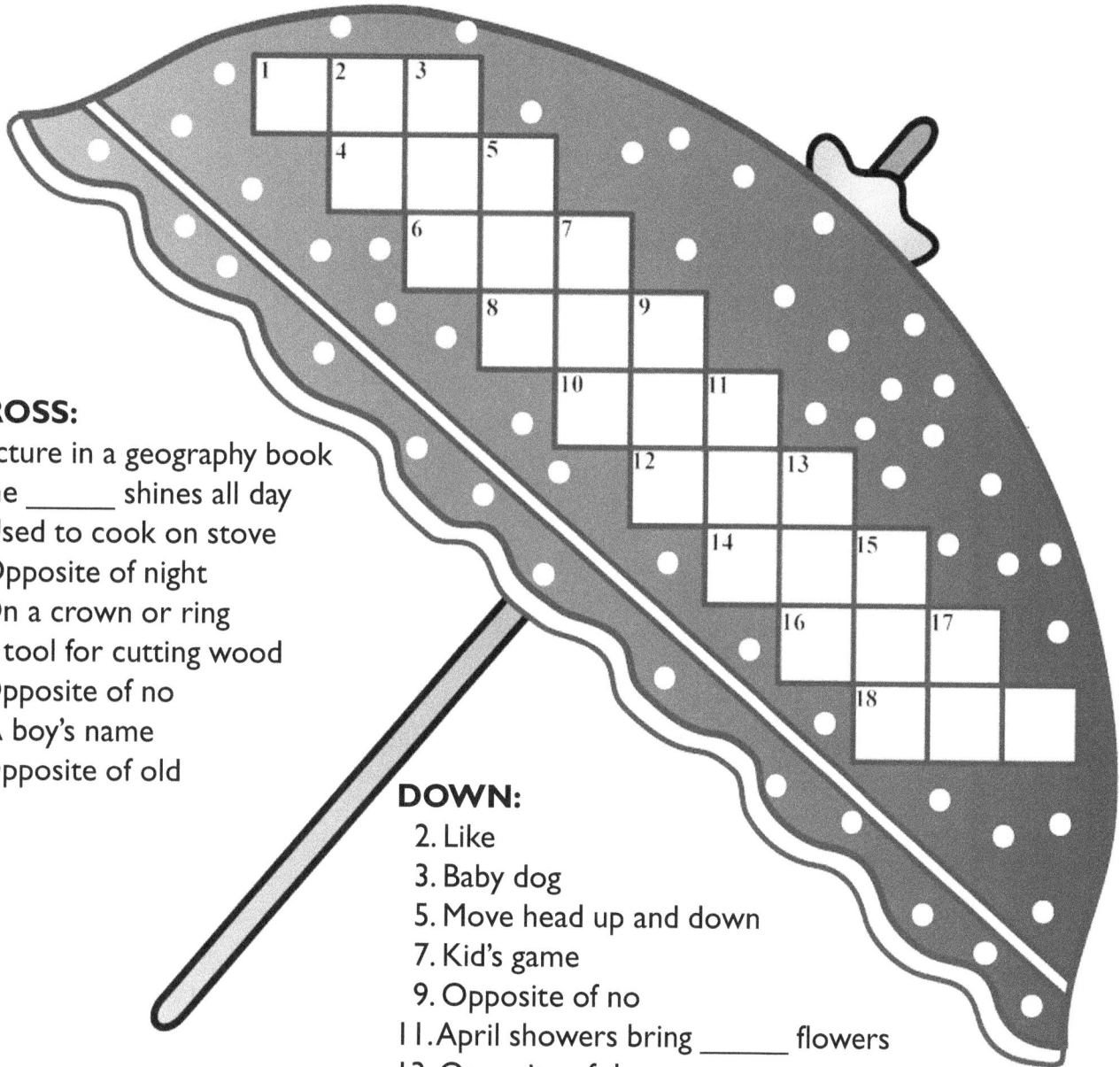

ACROSS:

1. Picture in a geography book
4. The _____ shines all day
6. Used to cook on stove
8. Opposite of night
10. On a crown or ring
12. A tool for cutting wood
14. Opposite of no
16. A boy's name
18. Opposite of old

DOWN:

2. Like
3. Baby dog
5. Move head up and down
7. Kid's game
9. Opposite of no
11. April showers bring _____ flowers
13. Opposite of dry
15. Dad's boy is his _____
17. _____ a name I call myself

POSSIBLE WORDS:

as, day, pup, map, May, me, new, nod, pot, pup, saw, son, sun, tag, Tom, wet, yes

Tea Party

Find the top view for each teapot. With a pencil and ruler, draw a line from each teapot to its top view.

1

2

3

4

5

6

7

8

9

10

Springtime Angel Bear

Grab your favourite colour pencils or crayons, and have fun colouring this beautiful springtime angel bear!

Tic-Tac-Toe

Find a friend, grab some pencils, and have fun playing Tic-Tac-Toe!

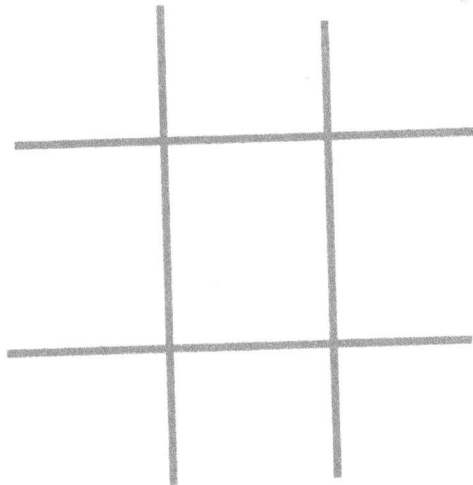

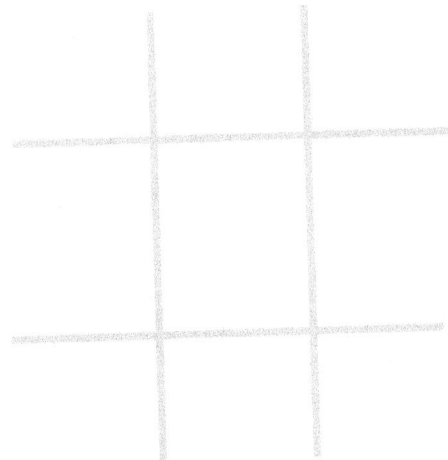

Flowers and Butterflies Sudoku

Using your colour pencils or crayons, complete the puzzle below. An image must appear only once in every 2x2 square, row and column.

Floral Shadows

Look carefully at each group of flowers on the left. Using a pencil or colour pencil and a ruler, draw a line from each group of flowers to its shadow.

A.

1.

B.

2.

C.

3.

D.

4.

April Showers – Scrambled Words

How many of these springtime words can you unscramble? Hint: the first letter of each word is capitalized.

1. Srignp _____

2. rdaipnsRo _____

3. hsorweS _____

4. luCdos _____

5. armelUbl _____

6. edluPds _____

7. phasSl _____

8. aoinRtosB _____

9. ocaRniat _____

10. drnThue _____

Insect Party

Complete the insect puzzle below. Draw a symbol (square, star, triangle or circle) next to each puzzle piece to identify where each piece goes.

PUZZLE PIECES:

Springtime Mystery Message

Find and circle the letters of each of the words below, using a pencil. Once you have completed the puzzle, the remaining letters will reveal a secret message that's just for you!

D	W	S	D	U	B	S	P	R	P
L	A	O	K	R	A	P	I	N	A
I	Y	F	L	N	I	B	O	R	N
R	A	G	F	L	Y	N	N	U	S
P	M	T	U	O	E	I	M	E	I
A	F	T	U	N	D	Y	A	T	E
T	H	S	A	P	L	I	N	G	S
E	N	E	R	G	Y	E	L	P	A
S	R	E	W	O	H	S	R	S	K
M	A	R	C	H	F	R	E	S	H

APRIL	ENERGY	MAY	ROBIN	SUNNY
BUDS	FRESH	PANSIES	SAPLINGS	TULIP
DAFFODILS	MARCH	PARK	SHOWERS	YELLOW

Mystery Message (22 letters, 6 words): _____

_____

Connect The Dots – What Am I?

What am I? Can you guess? Using a colour pencil or crayon, connect the dots, in order, from 1 to 58, and see if you guessed correctly. Now, colour your picture using your crayons or colour pencils.

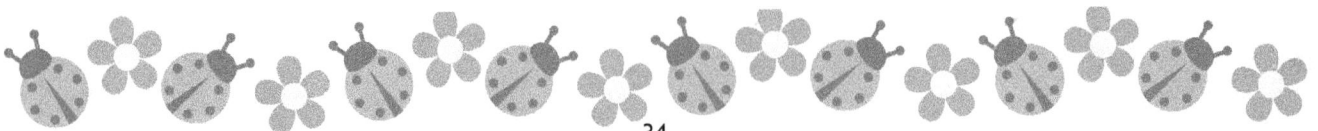

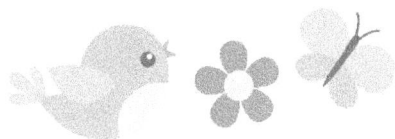

What I Love Most About Spring

What is your favourite thing about Spring? Using your colour pencils or crayons, create a drawing below of what you love most about Spring.

Cracked Shells – The Eggs

Look at each egg. Then, on the next page, find the piece of shell that goes with each egg. Write the letter of the shell piece under the matching egg.

1. _____   **3.** _____   **5.** _____

      2. _____   **4.** _____   **6.** _____

7. _____   **9.** _____   **11.** _____

      8. _____   **10.** _____   **12.** _____

Cracked Shells – The Shells

Match the shells to the eggs on the previous page.

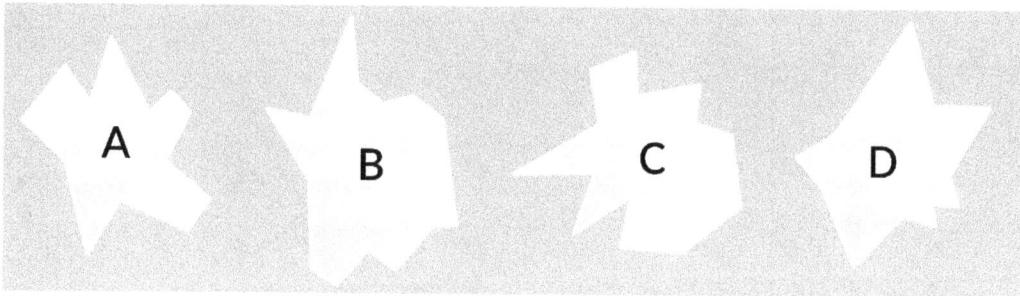

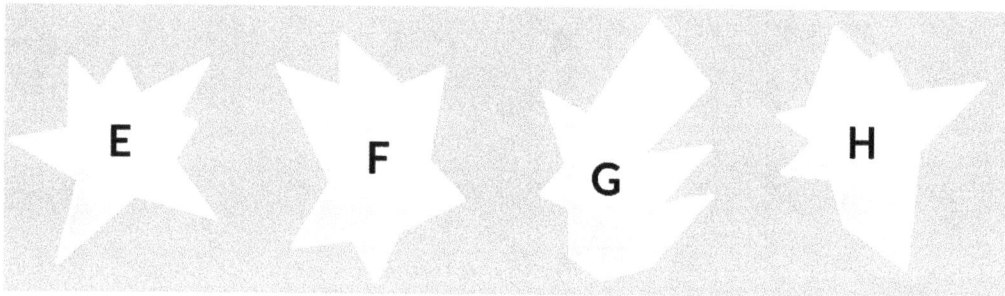

Birdhouse Village

Using a colour pencil or crayon, help every bird get back to the Birdhouse Village.

Floral Heart For Spring

Grab your favourite colour pencils or crayons, and have fun colouring this beautiful floral heart!

Fluttering Butterflies

Grab your favourite colour pencils or crayons, and fill in the blanks using one of the Butterfly images numbered 1 to 5. Next to each number in the grid, write the number of the missing image. There should only be one of each type of picture in each row and column.

Spring Zigzag Word Search

Have fun finding the words in this Zigzag Word Search Puzzle. Words go left, right, up down, but NOT diagonally. They can bend at a right angle. When you are done, there should be no unused letters, and each letter is used only once. Ignore spaces. To get you started, I've found the first word. Have fun!

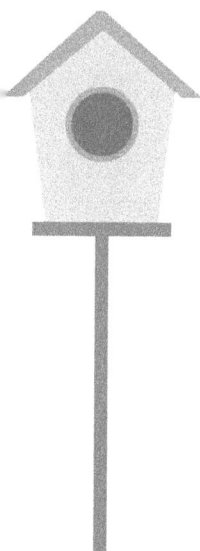

A	P	R	I	S	U	N	L	G	R
S	U	E	L	T	H	G	I	S	E
E	L	S	S	U	O	H	D	O	E
E	B	K	E	F	B	I	R	W	N
D	S	Y	N	R	E	S	S	I	G
L	T	S	E	E	N	G	G	N	R
I	N	G	S	S	H	A	S	S	A
B	C	H	N	E	D	R	M	A	Y
L	R	A	M	H	T	W	O	R	G
O	S	S	O	M	Y	O	U	N	G

APRIL	GARDEN	SEEDS
BIRDHOUSE	GREEN GRASS	SOWING
BLOSSOM	MARCH	SUNLIGHT
BLUE SKY	MAY	YOUNG GROWTH
~~FRESHNESS~~	NESTLINGS	

Tic-Tac-Toe

Find a friend, grab some pencils, and have fun playing Tic-Tac-Toe!

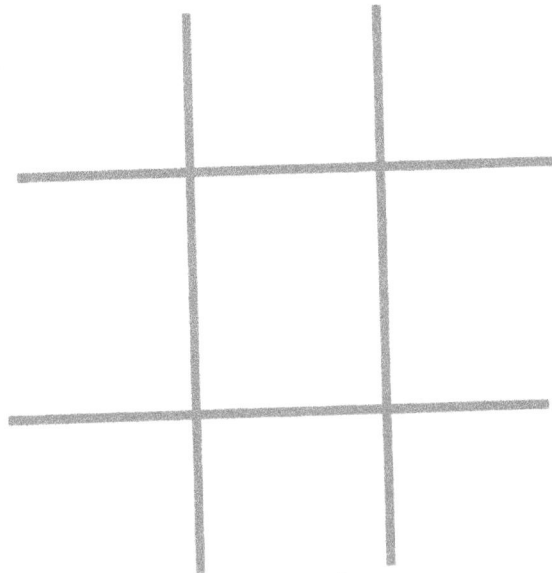

Springtime Birds

Grab your favourite colour pencils or crayons, and have fun colouring this beautiful springtime picture!

Connect The Dots – Sunny Day

What am I? Can you guess? Using a colour pencil or crayon, connect the dots, in order, from 1 to 50, and see if you guessed correctly. What did you create? Now, colour your picture using your crayons or colour pencils.

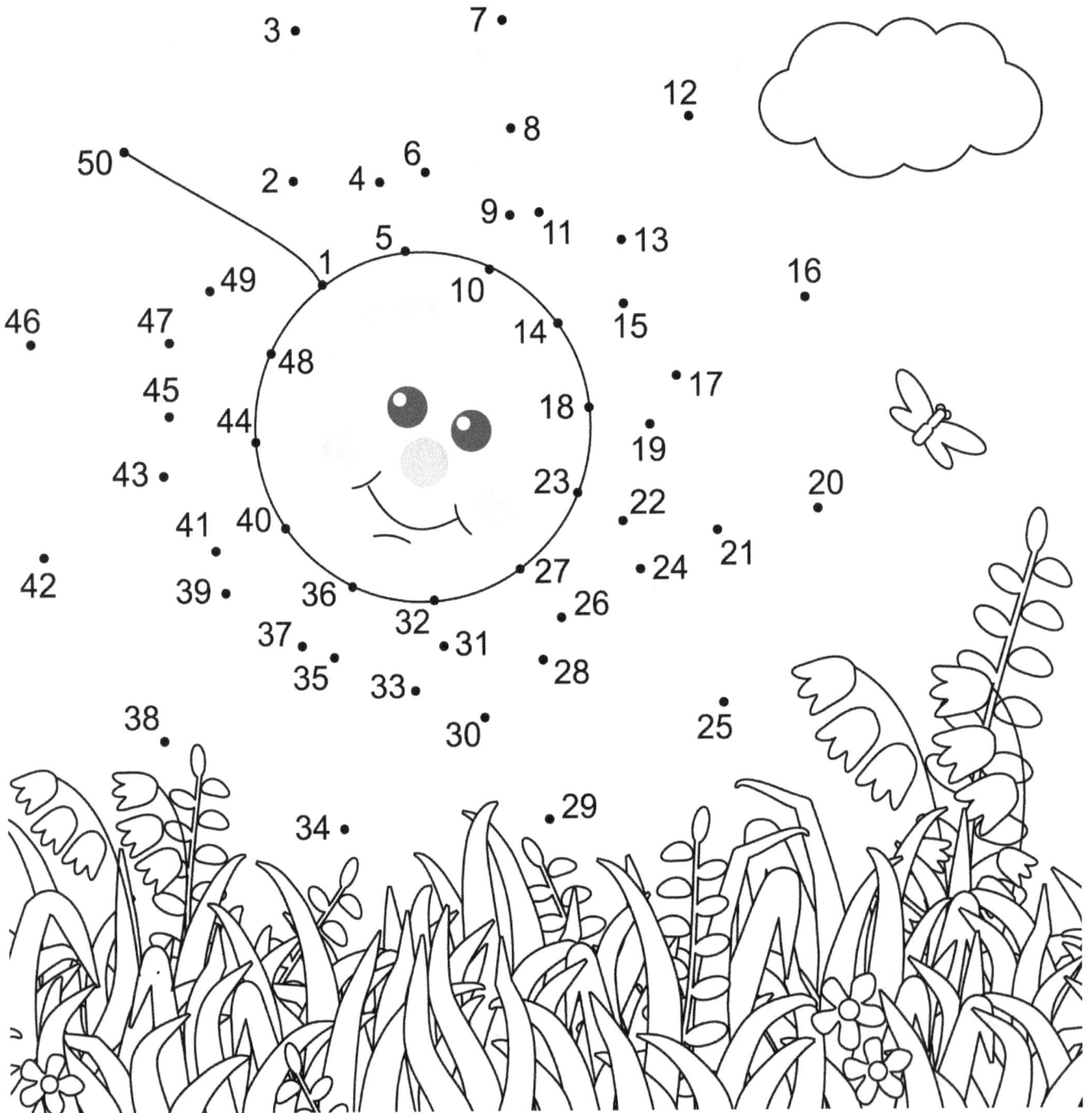

3
7
12
8
50
2   4   6
9
5   11   13
49   1   10   16
46   47   14   15
48   17
45   18
44   19   20
43   23   22
41   40   24   21
42   39   36   27   26
37   32   31   28
35   33   25
38   30   29
34

For The Birds

Using a pencil and the hints below, complete the Crossword Puzzle. For additional clues, be sure to look at the list of possible words.

DOWN:

1. This bird pounds it beak into wood to find insects
3. Birds that mimic the sounds of other birds
4. A blue bird with a crest on its head

ACROSS:

2. A small bird that eats nectar
5. A red bird with a crest of feathers on its head
6. A bird that typically has a brownish red breast

POSSIBLE WORDS:

blue jay, cardinal, hummingbird, mockingbirds, robin, woodpecker

Spring Flower Pots

Look carefully at each row of potted flowers. Draw a line from each row of potted flowers to its mirror image. One row does not have a mirror image. Find and circle the row that does not have a mirror image.

1

2

3

4

5

Flower Pot Maze

Using a pencil or colour pencil, make your way through the flower pot maze. Begin at the "START" point, and make your way through the maze until you get to the "End" point.

Start

End

Find 15 Differences – Part 1

Look at this picture and the one on the next page. Can you find 15 differences? Grab your favourite colour pencils or crayons, and circle the differences you find!

Find 15 Differences – Part 2

Look at this picture and the one on the previous page. Can you find 15 differences? Grab your favourite colour pencils or crayons, and circle the differences you find!

Spring Mega Sudoku

Using your colour pencils or crayons, complete the puzzle below. An image must appear only once in every 3x3 square, row and column.

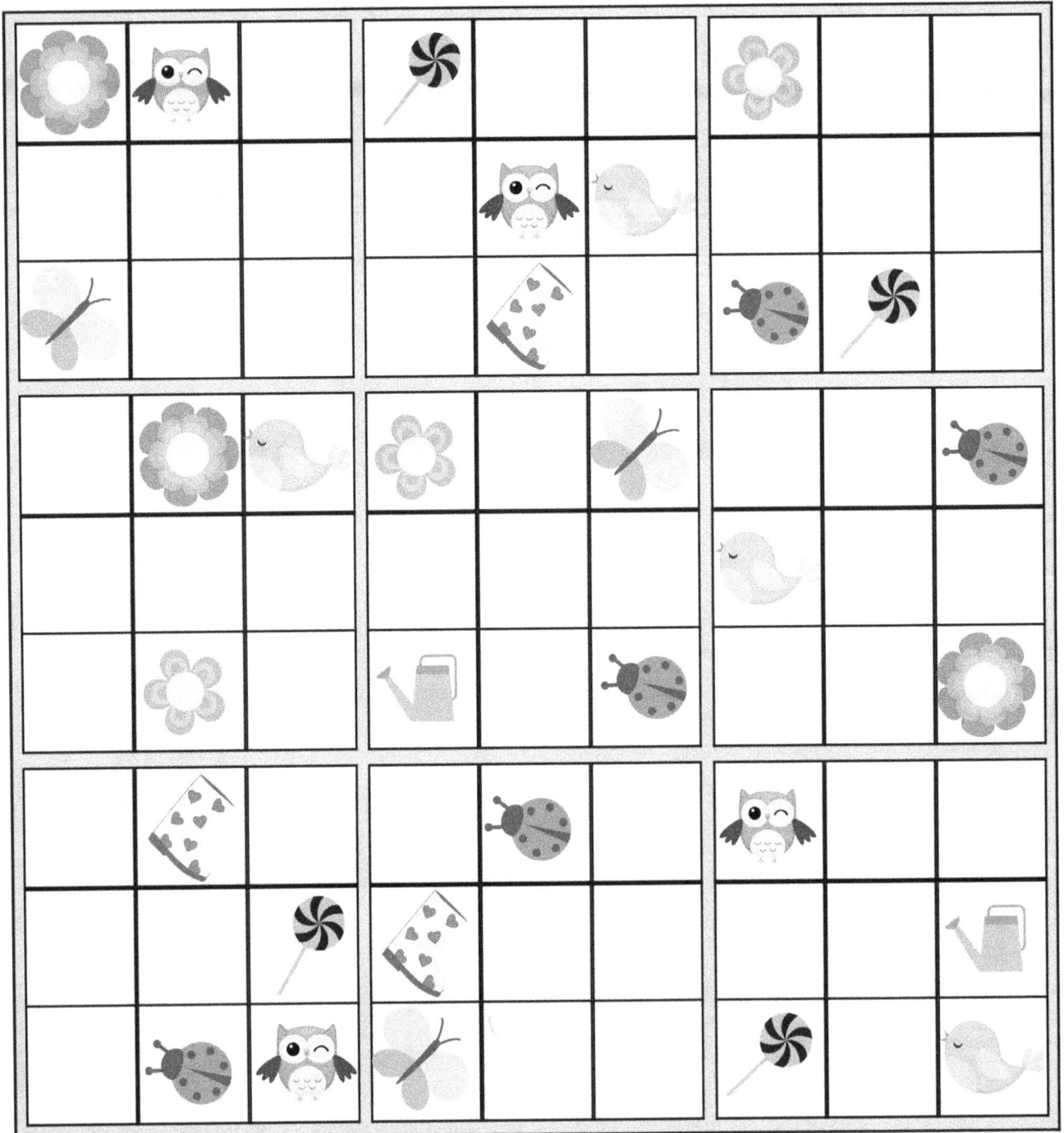

Owl Memory Game

Examine this picture carefully. Then turn the page, and see how many questions you can answer without looking back at the picture!

Owl Memory Game – Questions

Now that you have examined each item on the previous page, let's see how many questions you can answer without peeking at the picture.

1. How many owls are in the picture?

2. How many owls have both eyes closed?

3. How many owls are winking?

4. How many owls are facing right?

5. Where is the owl that looks angry (top, middle or bottom row)?

6. How many owls look sleepy?

7. One owl has an eyeball bigger than the other. Which row is he in (top, middle or bottom)?

I Love To Draw

What do you love to draw? Create one of your special drawings
below using your colour pencils or crayons. It can be anything at all!

Umbrella Maze

Using a pencil or colour pencil, make your way through the umbrella maze. Begin at the "START" point, and make your way through the maze until you get to the "End" point.

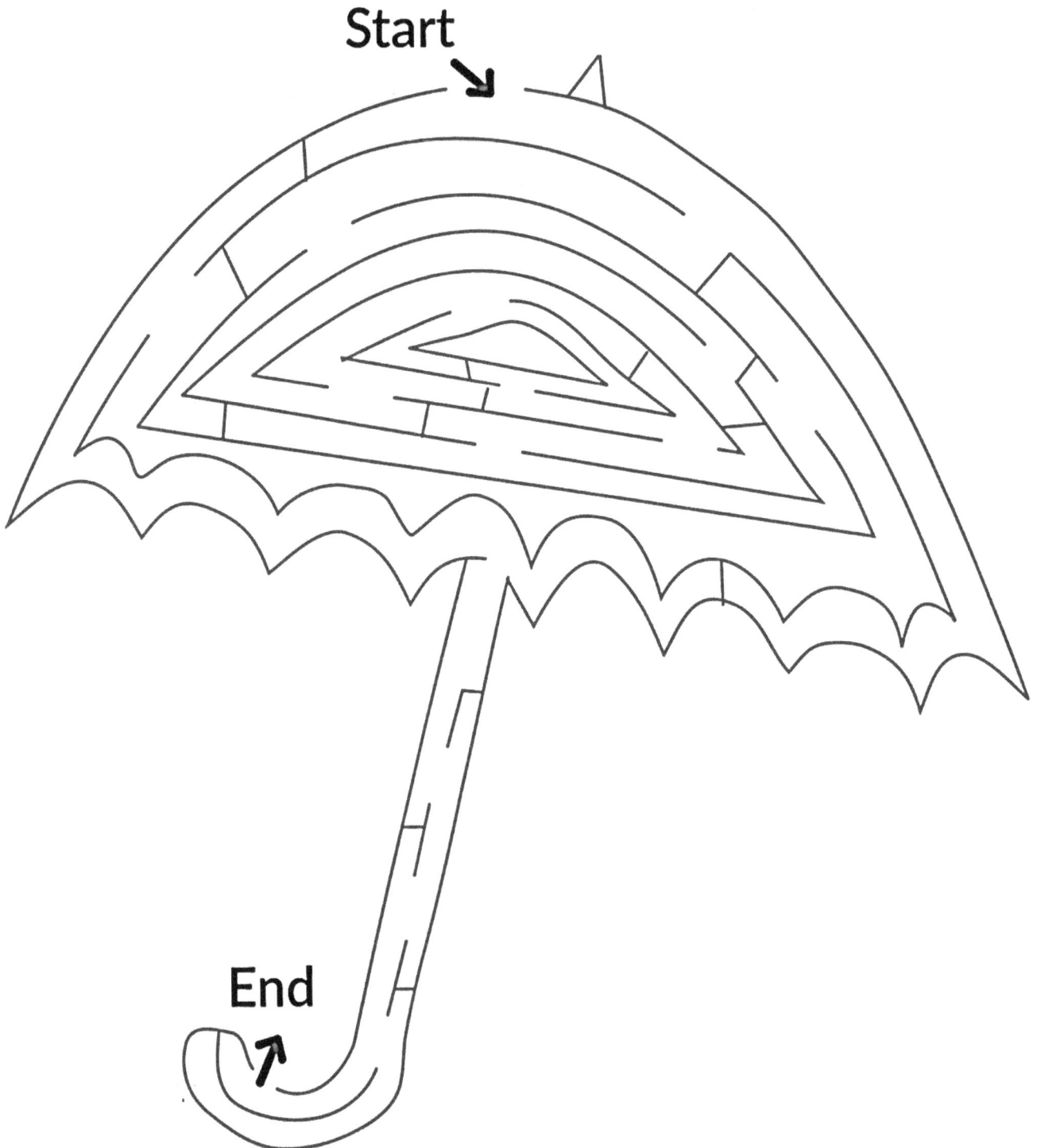

Start

End

Floral Splendor

Grab your favourite colour pencils or crayons, and have fun colouring this spectacular floral!

Floral Mystery Message

Find and circle the letters of each of the words below, using a pencil.   Once you have completed the puzzle, the remaining letters will reveal a secret message that's just for you!

H	P	R	E	W	O	L	F	N	U	S	A
P	Y	O	A	S	L	I	L	Y	P	E	R
U	I	D	I	I	E	S	U	N	E	S	E
C	R	L	R	N	N	S	A	N	O	O	B
R	I	D	U	A	S	O	O	W	N	R	R
E	S	A	T	T	N	E	G	R	Y	M	E
T	L	I	L	A	C	G	T	E	E	I	G
T	D	I	H	C	R	O	E	T	B	R	Y
U	G	A	R	D	E	N	I	A	I	P	S
B	N	O	I	T	A	N	R	A	C	A	I
N	O	G	A	R	D	P	A	N	S	R	A
B	A	B	Y	S	B	R	E	A	T	H	D

BABY'S BREATH	DAISY	IRIS	PEONY	SNAPDRAGON
BEGONIA	GARDENIA	LILAC	POINSETTIA	SUNFLOWER
BUTTERCUP	GERBERA	LILY	PRIMROSE	TULIP
CARNATION	HYDRANGEA	ORCHID	ROSES	

Mystery Message (11 letters, 3 words):

To grow, flowers need _____

I Love Fairies!

Girl's Activity Book

Don't miss any of the Kids' Activity Books.

Check out this sneak peek of:

See all of our **Activity Books and Journals**
at:
www.DiscoverYourPowerStrategies.com/JournalWithMyKids

I Love Fairies!

Girl's Activity Book

Sneak Peek!

Kids' Activity Book Volume 9

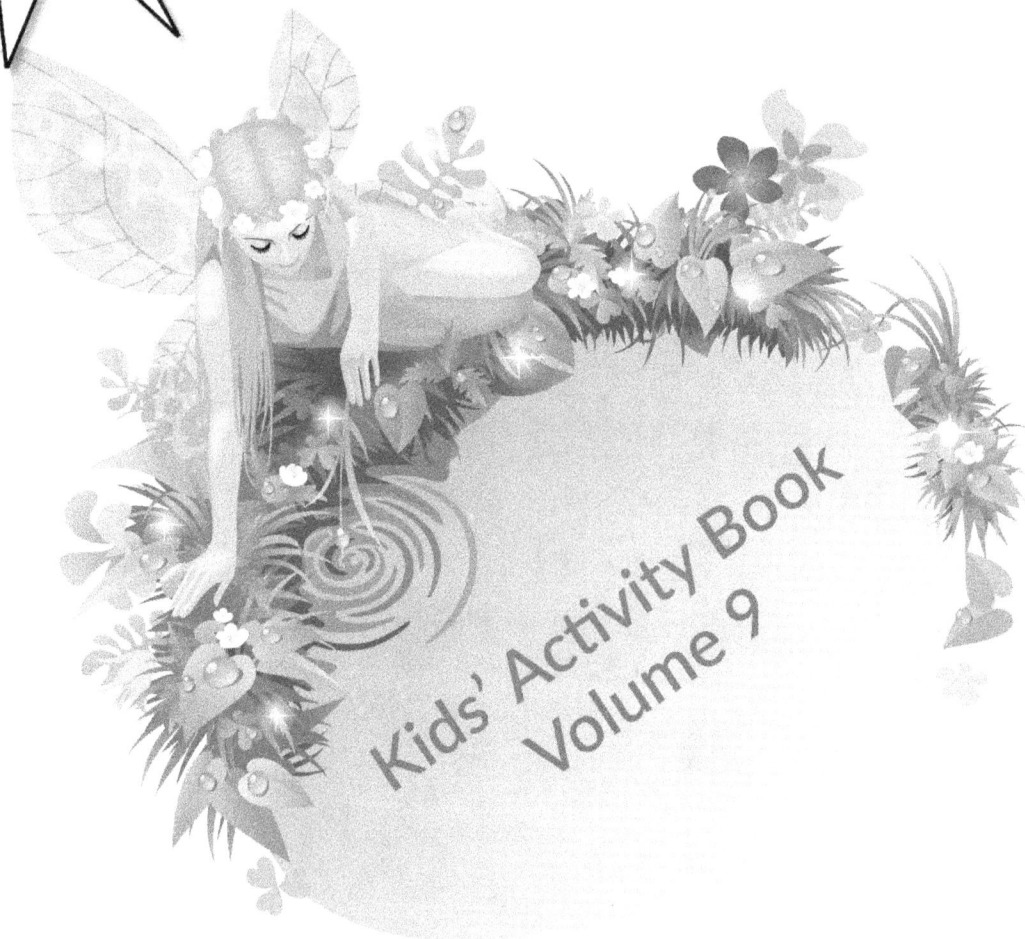

Sherley Grace

simply DONE PUBLISHING

Montreal, Quebec Canada

Welcome To The Fairy Kingdom!

Terri the Tour Guide Fairy would love to welcome you to the Fairy Kingdom! Using your crayons or colour pencils, colour this beautiful fairy castle.

Tooth Fairy Maze

Trixie, the Tooth Fairy needs your help! She needs to bring Sarah's tooth to the Tooth Depot. Will you help her? Using a pencil or colour pencil, help Trixie find her way through the maze, from Sarah's bedroom to the Tooth Depot!

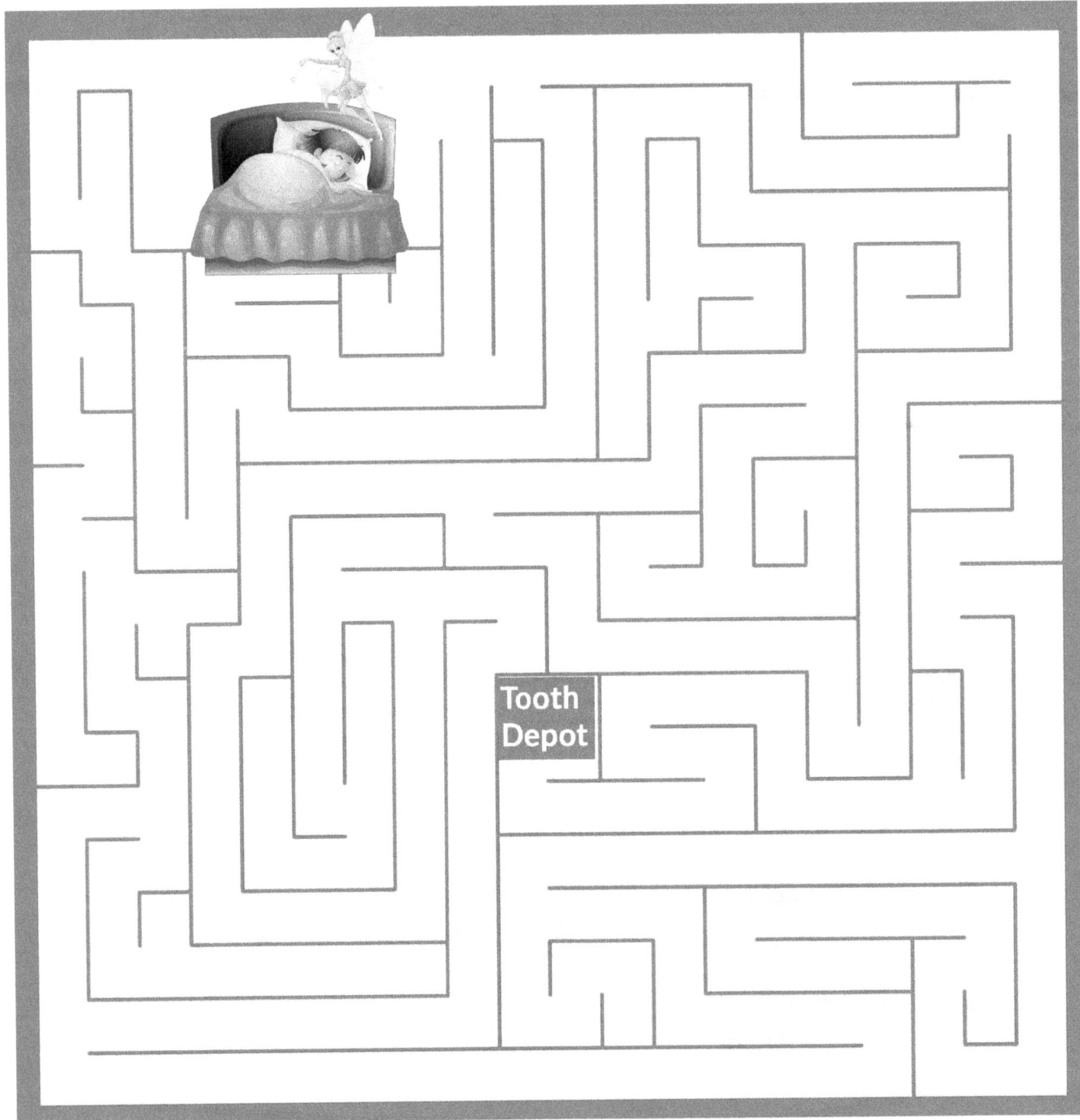

Tooth Depot

Get Your Copy Today
"I Love Fairies! Girl's Activity Book"

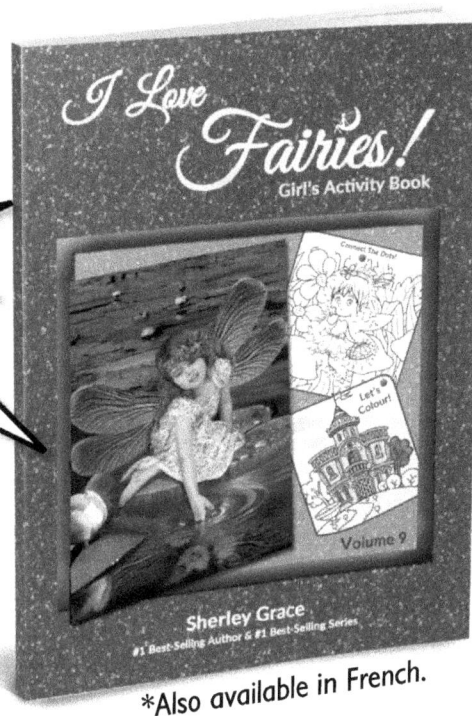

With ALL NEW Activities

Also available in French.

Meet and have fun doing activities with **Anna the Animal Fairy, Trixie the Tooth Fairy, Chrissy the Christmas Fairy** and many others! Find your way through **mazes**, **colour** beautiful, magical pictures, solve **puzzles**, discover **secret messages**, and much more!

Boy's Activity Books Also Available!

See all of our Activity Books at:
www.DiscoverYourPowerStrategies.com/JournalWithMyKids

Meet The Author

Sherley Grace is a #1 Best-Selling Author, Speaker and Award-Winning Business Coach.

Sherley is the CEO of simplyDONE Publishing and founder of DiscoverYourPowerStrategies.com.

She is the author of "*The Mother-Daughter Journal Series*", "The *Mother-Son Journal Series*", and the #1 Best-Selling *"I Love!"* Activity Books Series for kids.

She is also author of several soon-to-be-released books, including *"The 4-Figure Payday"*, and the children's picture book, "Sarah Bianca Visits the Animal Hospital", which she is writing with her young daughter.

After a 25-year career in human resources and leadership coaching and development, Sherley left the corporate world and started her coaching and consulting business.

Sherley empowers women to "Stand Up, Step Up and Stand Out", write and publish their books and connect with those who mean the most to them, so they can grow their business and create a legacy and the impact they desire.

Sherley lives in Montreal, Canada with her husband and children.

www.ingramcontent.com/pod-product-compliance
Lightning Source LLC
Chambersburg PA
CBHW081636040426
42449CB00014B/3345